Where is Home?

NANCY DUPUIS
THE WRITER IN ME

Order this book online at www.trafford.com
or email orders@trafford.com

Most Trafford titles are also available at major online book retailers.

Print information available on the last page.

ISBN: 978-1-4907-9505-8 (sc)
ISBN: 978-1-4907-9506-5 (hc)
ISBN: 978-1-4907-9507-2 (e)

Library of Congress Control Number: 2019906926

Trafford rev. 05/03/2019

 www.trafford.com

North America & international
toll-free: 1 888 232 4444 (USA & Canada)
fax: 812 355 4082

CONTENTS

Preface vii

Chapter 1   Lessons Learned.. 1
Chapter 2   The Master Does Have a Plan for Me 5
Chapter 3   The Best Trip Home Ever 8
Chapter 4   Love and the Emotion It Brings With It 10
Chapter 5   Music, a Way to Communicate........................... 17
Chapter 6   The World is Hurting.................................. 19
Chapter 7   Pushing Too Hard 20
Chapter 8   Returning Home 21
Chapter 9   It's Not Good-bye! 23
Chapter 10 Where is Home? 24
Chapter 11 Where am I Meant to Be? 27
Chapter 12 Bewildered 29
Chapter 13 Scared 33
Chapter 14 A Quiet Time 34
Chapter 15 A Time of Reflection 35
Chapter 16 A January Morning..................................... 36
Chapter 17 Done.. 37
Chapter 18 No Closure 40
Chapter 19 Leaving 41
Chapter 20 63 Days on the Road and Then Some..................... 48
Chapter 21 Home, Maybe Not....................................... 52

Author's Note.. 55
Acknowledgements... 57

PREFACE

Dreaming of a dress – fitted, hugging my soul; oh, and a hat, I have just the perfect one!

*But wait, my dream **has** come true as I wait to walk down the aisle, my wedding vows firm in my hand;*

"A kiss is only a kiss until you find the one you truly love, a hug is only a hug until you find the one meant just for you; a dream is only a dream until it actually comes true.

For it was not into my ear you indeed whispered, but deep into my heart. It was not my lips you kissed but actually my whole soul and being. It has been said love is not about finding someone to live with, but finding someone you know you can't live without. Thus, my journey back home. I didn't want to live without you.

It is also said that every woman's heart has different instructions and that they are written through her actions and also through her tears. She just has to find someone who cares enough to read them, and with you I truly have. I love you so!"

The wake-up alarm on my iphone shatters the stillness of the morning – reality, it's just a dream;

CHAPTER 1

Lessons Learned

What has made him this way? It was like there was some sort of barrier to feelings not expressed or lived, no commitment ever. I have to believe he did want me – some need he wouldn't admit, at least not out loud. Circumstances prevented that, and his frustrations showed when I vented mine. I couldn't live nor love like that – not touching, not being there with him. The pretense got to be too much. I so longed for time spent together, the real thing. I kept giving him chances, made all kinds of excuses for him. I now realize I was giving him the power to continue on thinking I would never walk away. Towards the end, he was so out of control; was it a manifestation of everything else going on in his life?

I knew it couldn't end well, but I deluded myself into thinking it would get better. I threw all caution to the wind, not leaving any room for my usual common sense to kick in. Why did I not pay attention to his actions? That would have told me so much. My close friends cautiously told me over and over, some not so subtly to move on. I chose not to listen, I was stubborn - all I ever wanted was some straightforward answers. And, I told myself, they did not understand the whole situation as I did. I do realize that I was likely hungry for the attention of any man when I met him – did he prey on that vulnerability? I am ever so grateful that I did not lose my close friends during this process and that they stood by me, not understanding completely but always there for me.

I sure loved the not knowing what he would do or say next, his effervescent nature – a very fun-loving guy bringing me to new heights I had forgotten existed. But then it went to a dark place, a place I was no longer comfortable with. Simple things like those occasional hugs should have told me something was not right. I didn't get excited. I was just responding. I kept brushing that thought aside but every once in a while the thought would come back, haunting me that this wasn't right, nor was he the one. As I wrote in my earlier memoir, "Begin Again", I must remember always that a false sense of pleasure invariably turns into pain. How easily though, I fell over and over for his charm, once more letting him control my complete being. Was this in actual fact some sort of abuse? I often think about that very question.

My world kept crashing. I was always tired of having to be careful as it was an affair of sorts, and too many of my friends knew who he was and even those who didn't – all would have been so shocked.

I was so hurt, over and over. Eventually I was finished, but oh, not yet - one more thing to do. I had threatened many times to blow the whistle, but I hadn't actually went through with it. What did I really want by telling her? I wanted him to wake up and smell the roses, if what he had said was true, then, he should have ended it long ago and moved on with whomever. Who was he kidding, me or more to the point, himself? My gut instinct tells me he was playing us both for fools and doing who knows what with whom else. So sad, for everyone that was caught in that web of deceit. At the end of the day, his actions told it all – lashed out at me in anger at what I'd done, when it was of his own making. There was still no acceptance on his part for anything that had taken place. Was it vengeance on my part? I don't think so. It was a cleansing for myself that she finally knew how he had belittled her so many times. She deserved to know. Whatever happened after that was up to them.

I still question the age difference, a man in the summer of his life, me I suppose in the autumn of mine. I wonder sometimes what role the age difference really played in the outcome. Some would say and some did, that he led me on. We were both guilty – I was the licorice at the candy counter he couldn't have and he, the indulgence I allowed myself to have even though I knew deep in my soul that this could never be. I need to put this in my past, how? Somehow, I must close that door, and open the door to my future; take a deep breath and step through, ever so gently, but step through.

He consumed my everyday thoughts for so long, actually my every waking moment and I endured many sleepless nights as the months and yes, years slipped by – the essence of his being surrounded me. We were like individuals drawn together by chance - little did I know, a man of dark secrets very few would know of, sharing amongst ourselves only. I hoped for answers he was incapable of giving. I do believe I kept that door open for so long, due to my own vulnerability and the spark in the air – the charm, the excitement from the light in my eyes (my whole face would light up when I thought of him). I still say "why me?" from time to time. What was I to him, I will never know. A loss for all concerned; shattered pieces of our lives, the tears, the anger, the fear at what we were doing to each other by remaining stuck in this make believe world that could never be.

After my inquisitiveness getting the better of me one weekend and probably of my common sense, I wanted to see what had happened to them in the past few months, in order to be prepared for any unplanned meetings in the future, especially if I came back to the same small town, so check social media I did. Sadness prevailed in my mind once I opened his page – single once again (or perhaps not), however no traces of his life with her remaining, and her page indicating she had been hurt but was moving on; actually her profile picture showed her in the arms of another. In the end, he lost through his own mistakes; perhaps this is of no matter to him. In a way we are even, I suppose. I enabled him to get out of a relationship he didn't seem to know how to do himself, and he injected some sort of infusion of living at another level into me.

CHAPTER 2

The Master Does Have a Plan for Me

Am I in a relationship, a real one this time? A compromise will have to be made eventually if he is the one – he has a life there that I can't ask him to forego. I can go back, and adjust. I have adjusted all my life, especially during our military years, and actually thrive on change.

Oh, how to tell my friends of my plans – I love them to bits here and don't want to hurt them in any way. I can never repay the many kindnesses bestowed upon me, since I arrived here almost three years ago. Hopefully everyone will be happy for me, although I suspect somewhat surprised, because I've kept this latest development under wraps for quite some time. I wanted to be sure it wasn't my imagination or just some fun on the rebound. The first one I will tell here will be my friend who is like a sister to me for various reasons. We laugh, we cry, we plan; yes, we even shop. I am so far from home and these people have stepped in and become my second family in many ways. Ok, I have told her – had to spill the beans to someone. She was supportive, why didn't I realize she would be - my kindred spirit?

Am I now able to tell the gold from the tinsel? It is our turn, each of us deserving some true happiness, once again. We have each lost, each been hurt, and so the understanding goes deep. He shows respect for me, loves his family and all of nature it seems. It would almost appear that our lives are mirrored, even the fact that we both lost our partners to the same cause. He is a gardener, and has a hobby he pursues with great passion. He seems a gentleman - my faith is restored once again. It's truly the little things that matter – he calls me by name – I love the possibility of being with the right one this time. I am learning though, that the so-called dating game is very different from when I was in my late teens. Mid- life brings with it, it's past.

I always tell myself "dare to dream,"! Every once in a while, I see a hummingbird outside and I sincerely believe it's my guardian angel telling me I'm on track. Writing has always helped me cleanse my soul. Tonight is no different. I sit here, cup of tea to one side of the laptop and my scribbled thoughts to the other. I wonder once I finish writing of the sadness of that affair gone wrong, how I will feel. To live it is one thing, but writing it in such a way as to not harm or belittle with my thoughts is quite overwhelming. But do it I must, to at least try to understand myself and the journey I am on. As beauty, they say happiness comes from within. I truly believe that. I have found that core of happiness again, something I thought would elude me for years again. The Master does indeed have a plan for me.

Slow down, calm down, savour the moments! My mind is going too fast, as usual. Stop. Let life evolve – embrace the getting to know each other, your own inquisitive nature and the kind, gentle nature of this one, always enquiring as to my day. Light-hearted banter, but really something much deeper – answers to questions that define who we are at this juncture of our lives. The remaining and somewhat looming question, I suppose is what has brought us to this point and what direction are we headed? I feel this is the person I could spend the rest of my life with. Is it too soon? I don't think so. I just have a really good feeling about this – please, I cannot be disappointed again. It's time to travel the distance and see if this is really the real thing – fingers crossed, double-crossed!

I do realize if it is, there will be compromises to be made. I realize this and I am sure he does as well. Would I go back? There appears to be truly a lot at stake. I feel deeply connected to the thought that my future happiness depends on the outcome of my visit home this time. This will be a different trip back, focusing on a few people close to my heart. I have to use this time wisely. Stay focused, reach out, and be honest. It is said distance is not an obstacle, but a beautiful reminder of how strong love can be. Let's hope so, for a bit anyways.

Oh, the excitement of the upcoming trip; the anticipation.

CHAPTER 3

The Best Trip Home Ever

The time spent in the Valley, the best time ever spent there, I felt like I belonged in this setting once again, but in a different way. I kept prolonging my return east. I wanted to stay in this man's company forever. I felt so comfortable sitting at his kitchen table chatting, like we had known each other for years, each sharing life's stories. Not disappointed. Things felt right, things felt comfortable. These hugs were the kind that made me want to stay in his arms forever. The answer to my earlier thoughts, would I go back? In a heartbeat, all he has to do is ask. I just want him to be sure of what he wants.

Back on the east coast now, I realize he is scared; I am not – stuck! What does the future hold for us? I am frightened but not intimidated. These feelings we each have will surely point us in a direction we can both live with.

It has been two months since I returned back East from my visit home to visit family and friends. He is offline this week due to computer problems and I am missing the frequent conversations through the messaging system something which he seems comfortable with. My feelings have not changed or diminished, if anything they have intensified. I think of him often throughout the day and wonder, stargaze, dream of what could be, or what might not be. I have to keep hope that things will work out, I so want them to. Have I deluded myself into thinking that this will be? I have no patience for this, I am so ready to jump in feet first and make this work. I am so sure of what could be. I am not foolish enough to not realize there would be hiccups along the way, but they are minor obstacles only, standing in the way only if we let them of real happiness.

CHAPTER 4

Love and the Emotion It Brings With It

Funny, I often think of the three men who have touched my life over the years; – my husband of 34 years, whom I think of only periodically now. It's been years since his passing, and as they said, "time does heal". "He's not coming back", my son so gently reminded me one day. How very true. Oh, if only he hadn't passed away when he did. Wishful thinking doesn't do anyone any good thinking of that scenario.

I awoke as normal this morning, checking emails and Facebook posts with my first coffee. One of my children had written an email letting me know her youngest child had started asking questions about Poppa. A bit of a struggle for her, I'm sure to talk to her child without a few tears and choking up. Photo albums were shared thus making the images seem more real in the eyes of her child. Another little grandchild had asked some of the same questions of me about a year ago, pretty blunt. "Is he dead?" Children say it like it is. I answered the questions, received a big hug and she went on her way. Did my heart good that day to realize she totally understood at such a young age what had taken place a few years before her birth and that she indeed would have been truly loved and of course spoiled by her Poppa if he was still here with us, as they all would have been.

Generous, loving, kind-hearted, modest, genuine, loyal were all words to describe Ray Dupuis, at his funeral in the spring of 2006.

Ray was quite interested in genealogy and just prior to his death, had started to write a bit of his own life story. He had seen this done somewhere prior on another individual's page and thought what a great idea, and thought everyone should do it, "even you, Nancy". Although the page was left unfinished, I believe you get a flavour of who the man was and of his deepest thoughts and concerns.

He was patriotic - devoting his life to serving his country - first in the Armed Forces, then as a public servant in Summerside, Prince Edward Island (PEI) and later in Ottawa, Ontario working for the Canada Revenue Agency. This devotion led to postings across Canada at Bases in Nova Scotia, Ontario, Alberta, British Columbia and Prince Edward Island - as well as a peacekeeping mission in Cyprus after receiving a promotion to Master Corporal. His work in the Forces taught him the importance of determination, patience, persistence, and working hard. It also taught him the importance of playing just as hard. He had a youthful spirit that was contagious and certainly showed it through his passion for music - being a big fan of Jim Croce, Alan Jackson and Diana Ross; and his favourite sports – badminton and fishing.

He was a family man first and foremost and an active member in his church community. He was a devoted father to Lisa, Jennifer and Michael. What follows is a beautiful depiction of the man Ray, was through the eyes of his children, written by them at the time of his passing:

"From the time we were little, Dad showed us how important we were to him by having a hand in every part of our lives. He was there to put the girls' hair in pigtails, he was there to sit on the couch and read us stories. He could draw pictures of anything we asked for. He took us to pet stores, and fishing and camping, and taught us to care about the plants and animals around us. We'd feed squirrels while camping, and plant flower gardens around the house every spring. He always made time to coach our sports teams and became a leader when Mike joined Beavers and Cubs, part of the local Boy Scout movement. And along with all the fun stuff, he made sure to give us a kick in the butt when we needed it. He gave us his time and we valued it so much that Jennifer would hide his Army boots after he'd been away in hopes that he wouldn't be able to leave again.

One of the best things about Dad was that he truly enjoyed the time he spent with kids. We were proud of the connections he made with all the kids in his life whether us, our cousins or our friends. Dad made our relationships a priority in his life. Mike has a happy memory of when they took the morning off of work and school to spend time with Mike's horse, even taking the time to stop by a store to pick up apples for her.

As we got older, Dad continued to teach us important things though his actions. He treated us with respect and gave us room to grow (along with a charter of rules and responsibilities on the fridge). He listened to us without judgement, offered advice and encouraged us to make our own decisions. He kept us safe while allowing us a bit of freedom. Lisa remembers the day she ran into her father at the mall when she should have been at school. He passed by with a smile but not a word, and he never brought it up at home. As each of us grew into adulthood our relationships with Dad continued to evolve. He offered us his support but never held us back. We knew he would always help if we needed it but felt good knowing Dad trusted our independence and was proud of the lives we were building.

Dad was so happy to welcome his grandchildren into his family. Even from far away each of the grandchildren had special relationships and happy memories of their Poppa. They didn't have a lot of time with him but they all know they have a lot of love from him.

Our Dad gave us all the things a Dad should give his children, the most important thing he did was give us an example of how to live a good life. If we can be as good a spouse, as good a parent, as good a friend, as good a person our Dad was, he'll have every reason to be proud."

Ray's story:

Born April 30, 1950

I was born in Sudbury Ontario and spent my childhood in Naughton, Ontario. In 1964 our family moved to Windsor, Ontario. This was a very difficult move for me as I had just completed Public school and was about to start High School. I was going from knowing everyone to knowing no one. As it turned out High school in the big city did not appeal to me and I ended up by dropping out half way through grade 11 and not completing my secondary education.

As Windsor was a factory town I started working in an automotive factory soon after dropping out of high school. Within the first year of my factory experience the automotive industry took a small down turn and I was laid off. During this time, work in the area was scarce. After causing my parents some grief I decided to join the Military.

I joined the Military in the fall of 1969 and started basic training at CFB Cornwallis, Nova Scotia in January of 1970. It was cold and miserable for the three months of training however, I was determined to complete the course. After basic training I was sent to CFB Borden, Ontario to await my trades training. Due to scheduling of courses, my training did not start until July of 1970. The three months prior was spent doing general duties around base Borden, another test of my patience. It is hard to believe that my son Michael is probably going through much the same today as I went through then!! Upon completion of my trades trading as an Accounting Clerk, my first posting would bring me to Ottawa in the fall of 1970.

My first posting landed me in the Accounting Unit at CFB Uplands, in Ottawa, Ontario which is now closed. I was provided with quarters right on base, as well as all the amenities of the times. There was the mess hall for dining, clubs for partying and gym facilities to help keep in shape. The last was not used as much as perhaps they should have been. But when you are young and full of it working out is not foremost on your mind, the clubs were the happening place!! So I partied pretty hardy for the first part of my career, then in the fall of 1971, I met the love of my life Nancy McKenzie, on a blind date no less. We were married on August 5th, 1972. On May 1st, 1973 our first daughter was born, Lisa Marie Dupuis. The next summer, with my promotion to Corporal, came our first posting as a family.

In the summer of 1974, we were posted to a small radar site, CFS Lowther. The station was in the middle of nowhere, about 30 miles from Kapuskasing to the east and 30 miles from Hearst to the west, in Northern Ontario. At this time postings to small radar sites were limited to two years. We took a trip to Kapuskasing in search of accommodations until our new home became available on base. We located a small trailer in a small town east of CFS Lowther called Opasatica. We spent a couple of months here and then moved to the base. We moved into a three-bedroom mobile home. On July 31st, 1975, the second addition to the family, Jennifer Lynn Dupuis, arrived. Shortly after Jennifer arrived we also decided to foster a child from the area. Loretta came to stay with us until our next posting, as the Children's Aid did not want the children from the area to leave. This kept Nancy very busy, as now, she had to look after Lisa, Jennifer and Loretta. The stay at CFS Lowther was most enjoyable and resulted in us making many new friends in the process. In the summer of 1976 came our next move.

The summer of 1976 saw us move to CFB Petawawa, Ontario. CFB Petawawa is located approximately 150 kilometres west of Ottawa.

As Petawawa is a hard Army base, I spent a lot of time away from home. There were numerous "field exercises" included trips to Borden, Ontario, Gagetown, New Brunswick and local field areas for military training. Training on weapons, first aid, and general army tactics filled most of the time spent here. I was promoted to Master Corporal in the spring of 1978 and in the fall of the same year, was sent to Cyprus on a peacekeeping mission with the 8th Canadian Hussars Regiment. While in Cyprus I learned that my family was growing once again. I made it back in the spring of 1979. My son, Michael Raymond Dupuis, was born on June 28th, 1979. We stayed at CFB Petawawa until the summer of 1981 at which time another posting arrived.

In the summer of 1981, our small family was sent to another radar site in the central interior of British Columbia known as CFS Baldy Hughes. The actual radar site is located approximately 30 miles outside of the city of Prince George deep in the wilds of British Columbia. We opted to live in the city rather than move onto the radar site. The site proved to be much similar to the previous radar site posting as the community was close knit. We developed many more close friends. Unlike the previous isolated posting at Lowther our stay here was extended to 5 years. In summer of 1985, I was promoted to Sergeant and transferred once more. It was sad to hear of the closing of all the small radar sites in Canada. These sites were real morale boosters due to the camaraderie and friendships that developed here.

(sadly, Ray's story was left unfinished so I have completed the logistics of the following postings as well as adding my own thoughts to this piece)

1985 saw us transferred to Ottawa, close to our families in Ontario, giving the children a chance to better know their grandparents, aunts, uncles and cousins. In 1990, we were transferred to Calgary, Alberta for a short period prior to Ray taking his release from the Armed Forces and moving as a family in the early winter of 1991 to Charlottetown, PEI where Ray had taken a position in the Reserve

Unit there. The following 8 years were spent in PEI, with Ray eventually gaining employment in the Canada Revenue Agency (CRA). In the fall of 1998 we moved to Ottawa, Ontario where Ray had taken a transfer with the CRA, remaining employed with the Agency until the time of his passing.

Your love of life lives on my friend, in each of the children and grandchildren. Your children have acquired your kind and generous heart, while the grandchildren are full of spunk and have a natural curiosity for life, much as you did. If I could have given you one thing in life, it would have been the ability to see yourself through my eyes.

The second man, was a time of exploration and learning that I could have those feelings again for someone else. Unfortunately, lessons were learned but took a bit of time for me to smell the roses.

But oh, to have had the special chance to meet the third man, the one who has truly stolen my heart and soul during this time in my life. I am truly in love, once more. I care deeply for this man, and so want the chance to show him that I do.

CHAPTER 5

Music, a Way to Communicate

Coming near the holiday season, I am now entertaining thoughts of returning home for a couple of weeks during the festivities. I so want to be with this man again, our almost nightly chats online have stirred my interest further and I can't wait to see him and be with him again. I find it remarkable that since the end of summer we have maintained our chitchats and how much I look forward to them. We have even went so far as to say, there is indeed meaning behind our friendship, both I'm now positive wondering where the journey is headed. This man loves music and loves to share some of his favourites or perhaps those fitting the occasion with me. I so look forward each evening to what song he will send my way. We have found a way to communicate over the distance. Not hearing from him when he is busy, has made me realize just how much I care.

What have I done? Have I pushed? The silence is deafening these last few days. I have some decisions to make soon as to whether I remain in the East for the winter or move back home, or even just go for Christmas for a visit? He had indicated in the last couple of weeks how much he had enjoyed the visit in the summer and that he indeed had big feelings for me in his own words. I should have asked then what that meant. Is it just a feeling, however huge that cannot be acted upon for whatever reason?

I am determined to get to that reason and deal with it. This story has too much value to it, to throw it away. I now realize I want this new maturity in life I've found in this man. The previous indiscretion and immaturity were just fluff, setting me up for what was to come.

CHAPTER 6

The World is Hurting

Friday, November 13, 2015 – the Paris massacres; my shock and disbelief as well as hurt at what I am seeing posted on FB by friends; is it bigotry or just fear?

Tuesday, March 22, 2016 – the Brussels massacres; will it never stop?

> `"I would like to be known as an intelligent woman, a courageous woman, a loving woman, a woman who teaches by being"*
>
> *- Maya Angelou*

I too, would like to be this person.

CHAPTER 7

Pushing Too Hard

OK, enough, pick up the phone and ask? The result was not what I wanted to hear, but much as I had expected. I had pushed too hard; we are not on the same page. One not willing to give up their life as they know it at the moment, the other too anxious to enjoy all life has to offer, now! We chatted for a long, long time and had an online conversation a half hour later. All is good. We remain friends and I'm sure always will. It is a totally different feeling this time, no anger at this person – just heartfelt wishing he could move past his inhibitions, allowing us both the opportunity of some enjoyment in life together in this moment. I must remember to take time and appreciate our similarities and also to respect our differences. I keep thinking about how different my life has become because of meeting this fellow; everything in my life as I knew it, has changed. So very wonderful! I enjoy so much the music links he sends my way on a very regular basis; such a soft, kind-hearted, tender man.

CHAPTER 8

Returning Home

I am not going home for Christmas, but am moving back home in the New Year. I have come to the realization that I am healed. I am a very different person than when I arrived in the East, three years ago. My trip back home this past summer, had left me wondering about many things. It feels good to have come to this decision, although a huge surprise to many. Not one I made lightly, for sure. This man has everything to do with my decision, yet nothing. I truly have fallen in love for a second time in my life and will certainly be happy to be closer to see how this story evolves. Hoping, fingers and toes crossed. But I'll be ok if we only remain friends. Friendships are to be valued, especially ones with such meaning. This and my Mom's deteriorating health have made me come to the realization it's time to go home.

Christmas Eve - the meat pie is cooling on the stovetop, now for a little rest before heading to the 4 pm service at church. I think we may have come through a bit of a disagreement of sorts this week. He was awfully quiet this week, and I was certainly missing the chitchat. I confronted him finally, with my thoughts on the various music, he had been sending me. I've kept a playlist of the various tunes and oh my, the lyrics seem to fit every occasion. Back on track, last night's choices seemed to be nothing different, just more of this man expressing his feelings through music, it would appear.

I can't wait to get home and talk to him in person about the last few months.

Christmas night; I can't sleep, thoughts tossing and tumbling, time to sit down and write. I am so restless - time seems to be standing still. I pack a couple more boxes, letting my thoughts drift as to what I am doing and why. What will be the outcome? No time to ponder - just put the plan into action. Go! I so want this man's arms around me again, encompassing my being. I know what that feels like and have missed it so, since that visit in the summer.

The Christmas season is emotional, always has been for me. All the expectations, the hype and pageantry, are a bit much to me. The true meaning seems so lost on most people. I have always struggled with other people's lack of understanding and at times am still perplexed. On different occasions I have helped at homeless shelters and soup kitchens, other times just quietly going along with the flow.

This year, as I head back home early in the New Year, I am deeply troubled as to a couple of my friendships. These two individuals are not aware that they were part of the reason I left home three years ago. I need to come to grips with how I will handle these friendships upon my return. Obviously it needs to be in a different way, for my own wellbeing. Why do I let them get to me? The good in me wants all to be friends, and to help all. I have to realize that some cannot be helped, they will always be stuck in their own thoughts and ways and no amount of chiding will ever change that. Again, it's me who has to change the way I handle certain situations. Easier said than done, but I must try to make the effort if I am to be free of these strangling feelings and anger of late as I deal with these individuals. It seems like we are never on the same page. I am the free-spirited Nancy; they, the same forever, set in their ways and especially their thoughts of how others should be.

CHAPTER 9

It's Not Good-bye!

January, the month of good-byes or so it seems; New Year's Eve was lovely, spent with the first people I met upon my arrival in Nova Scotia at their Bed & Breakfast, a few years ago to look for accommodations. There was lots of great food and drink and of course the recipe for crab apple liquor to bring back with me.

I reread my book. 'Begin Again" before setting out and was astonished to find that there were signs in that book of my healing and when that started to happen, as well as signs of my eventual return home.

Many are questioning why I am returning home. I forget I lead a pretty abnormal life to some, coming and going as I please, just letting each day be a new day. The few that do know why I am returning are fully aware how hard it is to leave the many friendships here and my overall love of the place. I am so lucky to have such truly supportive friends all across the country. It's so hard to say so long to some, as you wonder if you will ever see them again and if so what the circumstances will be like at that time.

CHAPTER 10

Where is Home?

The first weekend back home visiting in the town I had left a few years prior, I kept having these feelings of claustrophobia. Everything seemed so crowded, coming in on top of me. Was it because I had loved the wide openness spaces of where I had just left, or was it the old memories coming back to haunt me. I truly believe my body was telling me something. I am so glad I had made up my mind to live in an adjacent town this time round.

A funeral to attend the first week back – a relative of some of my late husband's family; sitting in the church that morning for the service I now have a deeper understanding of the differences between my religion and that of my husband; at least a little bit. I now get it when I think back to how he kept his own faith, even though he attended church in the later years with me and always was such an amiable sort to help out wherever and whenever needed.

So many new things to experience my first few weeks back; along with all the fun it seems there is always a bit of sadness too; a good friend's brother passed away this past week at a way too young age, some friends are getting older and with that comes adjustment in one's living, and just missing my close friends in the East. All reminders that life is fragile - take good care of it!

Wandering the streets of my new town, exploring and enjoying visits with my Mom and especially my littlest granddaughter have certainly brought a smile to my face. And of course the texts from friends back East checking in and checking up. I seem to keep calling here and back East "home". Where is home?

I took an afternoon recently and headed off to the movies – the movie 'Brooklyn', brought similarities to mind – girl leaves home, goes to NY, meets her love, goes home but soon returns to NY as that is where her heart lies. Me, I come home, meet someone I care very deeply for and upon returning home to the East last fall, realize that I could never be the same again – need to go back home; whether this is just a friendship or not, I would never forgive myself for not coming back to get to know this individual better.

Seems a bit odd, now – friendship on and off, hot and cold; I am now at a loss at the quietness this week; frightened, hurt, sad, angry, as I still have huge feelings for this individual. What's to come of this? Mixed messages I am having trouble understanding. Oops, then pops up when I need him most – more music coming my way; he's heard something on CBC and shares it with me. Love him, so! A truly kind, sensitive man! I am starting to have a deeper understanding of this man, and the time he makes for me in his thoughts.

As I told another friend this past week, I am fine alone, I always have been – however, this I think could be or have been something very special. Will I be content if it turns out just to be friendship? Will that be enough?

6-7 weeks back and troubled I am, time to clear my head and truly begin to really "live" here again!

I attended a function, reaffirmed in my mind, that I can't go back in time – ok to remain friendly, and touch base with friends on occasion, but remember to not let the past drag me down.

I spoke with a family member about past things that had gone wrong in our immediate family and that were beyond repair. Once the word has been spoken, it can never be taken back. Too much hurt has existed way too long in my heart from cruelties dealt by others.

I wrote a quick note, dropping it in the mail with a few thoughts, needed to get it out – the mixed signals last summer of his thoughts and then of the emotions and carrying on throughout the fall leading up to my move back; the ghosts of our pasts, troubled eyes and what they tell the world.

I am overwhelmed by the realization that I feel very lonely here this first few weeks back, much more lonely than I was when I lived in the East. It's a case, I suppose of returning to something that you are no longer considered a part of and trying to find your piece in the puzzle. You are always that person "from away".

Then, a rude awaking so to speak – had the opportunity to have my eyes opened once again, met some couples this past week, who lived the glamourous life it seemed, the two car garage, the lovely home with the perfect flower beds etc. Then I met a few single older women, widowed, or perhaps spinsters – certainly not living the grandeur life, but managing. Opened my eyes once again to life around me – I am not alone in this life; all have stories.

CHAPTER 11

Where am I Meant to Be?

What happens next? Dropping by for a quick visit, always entails a great chat and a cup of tea, or two; neither of us are ever at a loss for words, so much to talk about, catching up on all those years prior.

This is an emotional time of year for me, and oh how I can let loose – the season where we found out my husband's diagnosis, and then of his subsequent passing. In between all that numerous reminders are felt of his birthday, his late brother's birthday, and his brothers passing as well. Facebook seems so full of everyone's reflections during these times. I sometimes let them pass by with not much emotion; other times I let them upset me to the point of almost exhaustion.

Again this week, I am tormented by troubling thoughts of where I am meant to be? I still feel very lonely here – is it my own fault, what do I do to change that? Everyone is busy with their own lives and they were before I came back to town, thinking I was the centre of their universe. Just kidding, I do realize all that, I am just trying to find my comfort level in each day where I feel truly whole as a person again.

"What defines me? Who am I? Who do I want to be? I have to remember these are my choices, mine alone!"

I have to remember to not push so hard, not be so ready; sometimes others are not on the same page as me.

Then arrives the emotions of the spring – the shadow of sadness that pours over my being, never knowing when. I just have to ride it out, cry, cuddle up under the blanket and have a little sleep – my method of escape, I suppose. I am still stunned by the effect my late husband's birthday and anniversary of his death have upon me. Some years are more poignant than others, no reasoning behind that, just the years passing by and I suppose the impact of my thoughts at that moment in time.

CHAPTER 12

Bewildered

I am just "existing", again! What is my purpose in life? I have only been back 5 months and I am overcome with these feelings of frustration again. I am reminded over and over that all the things that drove me away from this part of the country, 3 ½ years ago, still exist. The only thing different is that I have fallen in love so deeply with another man from here. I have moved my Mom to long term care, I have answered the call to volunteering, and I am trying to be what everyone wants me to be. I am now entertaining thoughts of what to do next. Answer I think is to stay here for the next couple of years, give my Mom the benefit of my being near and helping out as needed, stay till the school reunion is over in summer of 2018, then set out on the next adventure. First and foremost this week will be to find some work to keep me actively engaged once again. I do not like this feeling of depression at what I have done. My relationship with this man has blown up in my face, over a disagreement. Live and learn, however if you can't voice your opinion, then what is the relationship worth in the end?

A few weeks later and things seem more positive. We are at least talking, a nice afternoon visit, always so much to chat about. We are never at a loss for words. I've pushed a bit again – I need to know where I stand. A friend reminded me yesterday that I shouldn't let this go on forever, missing out on other possibilities that await me. I can't go on like this forever; I hurt, I long for this man and to be his. I am not ready to let go just yet, I still feel a great love and connection to this man. Another evening of wondering what is to become of this?

A chat with a new friend today jolts me back to reality – this is not likely a good place to be, me wanting this man and not much return on the feelings. I cannot ever change what is. It is up to him to change the ways that are detrimental to his health and subsequently to his relationships not only with me, but with family and friends. After hearing more of his past today, and putting two and two together, I stretch out on the bed and allow those thoughts to filter through. Scary it is, to know someone you love is and maybe has been for a long time suffering alone.

Always one to take the bull by the horns so to speak, I jumped in my car and paid him a surprise after supper visit. He was doing his chores so I settled myself on the back step, steeling my nerves, waiting. He seemed happy enough to see me, sat and chatted for an hour or so, before going back to his chores. It is always that way, always made to feel welcome in his life at the house. I feel so comfortable there and happy. I always get a deeper understanding of just how busy his life is, but wonder where I fit, if I do?

A Sunday morning heading out for groceries, the car seemed to have a direction of its' own. With tears streaming down my face, I needed some answers; was there any hope of a future with this man? Or, should I retreat, head back to the East Coast and try to wipe this memory off the chalkboard of my life story?

Answers were again not what I wanted to hear – so I left sobbing my heart out in the car all the way back home. I cried on and off all day, throwing myself down on the bed a number of times that day, the pain felt coming from deep within. What was I to do next, people depending on me again to be here for "them" but myself not in a good place? This was starting to play havoc with both my physical and mental health, and I was smart enough to know, something had to give- this had to change, now! By evening, a message received to come and talk; we talked until the wee hours of the morning. The time since has given me a better understanding of this man and myself and how we do indeed enjoy each other's company. What the future holds is anyone's guess but I am now OK with that. My health has improved, I am not so dependent on what the future holds now, I am again enjoying each day of my life, and just relaxing and enjoying being in the moment.

The fall, my favourite season is quickly approaching. I am still pondering what I mean to this man and if it is enough for me? Laying low for a bit seems to have paid off. Again, a beautiful love song came my way this evening, at the end of his busy day. He tugs at my heart. I am his, when will he realize that or is this all there is?

Tonight, again the car seemed to take on a life and direction of its own. A previous time with this man and his comments had shot into my mind. My inner instinct proved me right. I am back home now, experiencing sheer contentment; an impromptu drop in, with a goodbye touch on my back as I was leaving. I thought on and off all evening about how much that touch meant to me – pure simplicity in the feel of a touch from a man I so love. That was enough tonight.

It took almost 6 months for me to bump into that other fellow and I am not surprised by my immediate reaction. Flee or stay? Stay I did, after battling for a few minutes that "take flight" feeling. I thought a lot about that brief encounter later on that evening, and how I have changed over the last few years, no longer lost in my feelings as to why my husband died and left me so alone; no longer bitter as to that brief fling and now so much in love again at this point in my life.

A gentle nudge from my friend, to get out there and get involved – "you are a people person" he had said. He knows me well. It didn't take me long to get moving, now finding some much needed balance in my new life here. It isn't complete yet, but I have to learn to give that time for now. I keep remembering comments from others to not let this go on forever – but I still believe there is hope. I cannot and will not move on while I am still deeply in love with this man – his actions provide me with enough hope to not want to end this just yet. I remain locked in my feelings, waiting for either the ultimate reward of spending the rest of my days with this man, or release. That extended trip home to visit last summer indeed set me up for what was to come even though the "unknown" at the moment.

CHAPTER 13

Scared

Is my Mom fading away? Almost 94, a trooper till the end! It appears some illnesses may have now rendered her bedridden. I now am also beginning to realize the full brunt of family issues surrounding my siblings and myself.

I am still very much in love, but oh so stubborn too – where do I stand with this man? We have our differences over things but I don't believe for one minute that this is over! It can't be as the feelings have run deep for way too long on both sides.

Those impromptu visits are absolutely the best! Dropping off books for a member of his family, dropping off a lovely old tablecloth I'd found at a second hand store, that so belonged in his house, always amazes me with the outcome. Such happiness that morning in a brief conversation in the yard; I felt the electricity still between us; it's still there! Admission on his part later on that evening that yes, indeed it's still there! I ponder the future, but am so in love – the warmth of this man's embrace has me feeling goosebumps still.

CHAPTER 14

A Quiet Time

A lull in my writing; life has come to a standstill, I am drained! My Mom, so very ill and in palliative care these past few weeks has left me just plain tired out. Everything else seems to have been put on hold till we somehow get through this sad time. A week or so before Christmas 2016 and somehow by God's grace, Mom is still with us, at least for today.

I have come to the conclusion, perhaps I am better off alone – it seems so hard some days to understand if this friendship of the last while is anything more than just that. This man is content it seems with his life the way it is – it's the times when we are together that leave me wondering and hoping that there is more. Only time will tell, I have come to the conclusion to live my life as it is here at the moment and see what happens next. I love my volunteering in the community, a huge part of my life and love the very special relationship I have with my littlest granddaughter who lives nearby.

CHAPTER 15

A Time of Reflection

New Year's Eve, 2016 – Mom is still with us, my love life still in pieces it seems, let's just turn the page tomorrow to 2017, please.

I am home tonight due to a snow storm and lots of time to reflect, I suppose. A wonderful evening was had a couple of nights ago with the man I so love. This love story is still ongoing. Impatient I am though to see what the future holds for us?

I am amazed my Mom is still here, some days better than others. That too has me questioning a number of things, especially when I consider myself a fairly religious person. I have trouble grappling with the pain and suffering to be endured by the individual and subsequently on those around them that love them so.

CHAPTER 16

A January Morning

The most pleasant of days this morning, being in the moment – picked up for a drive to visit his Mom and take her for a drive. I so enjoyed getting to know these two even better this morning and to see what makes their relationship as mother and son, so very special. And, to be part of their very special time - that meant a lot to me to be included.

I am certainly experiencing "Mom" withdrawal these past couple of weeks as a bug has hit the nursing home where she resides, so no visiting till the "all clear" is given. I have kind of a surreal feeling when every once in a while, I get the notion that this is a type of practice run when Mom will no longer be with us. There are tears in my eyes, even as I type this last sentence and come to grips with the finality coming.

Always a planner type of person, I usually need to have life planned out in front of me for at least the next year. But now, it's become so very different. Some days I feel lost and bewildered as to what do I do after my Mom passes? What will fill that void in my life? Will it be that man or will it be something else? I so want it to be that man for sure, but that remains strictly up to him. If not, I do know I will again have to move forward in true "Nancy" fashion – one foot at a time onto that next adventure!

CHAPTER 17

Done

The realization that this man does not need me in his life; my Mom has passed away; family has broken apart with a little one remaining a strong spirit, thank goodness. My heart yearns for peace.

I have spent the day volunteering with organizations where some are not pulling their weight and making it hard for others to continue to have faith in the organization. Time will only tell. I am stepping away for a while to let the dust settle, as the saying goes, not my monkey. But maybe it is, can I help, or is it too late for these organizations? Will they fold – have they outrun their life?

I look at friends or so-called friends on social media and wonder, am I really where I need to be or does something bigger await? I feel like I have been put to the test, but yet on the cusp of something very new.

I am torn, I want to be a friend still but he makes that impossible, retreating into his self at times, not letting the outside world in. I must remember I cannot fix this, only he can, whatever he chooses. My heart is broken once again.

My Mom's passing this spring has been rather surreal. I realize it was time for her to go, especially at 94, but still so hard to fathom her not being just up the road. I find myself many times since her passing, thinking "I must tell Mom that", only to realize she is truly gone. Tears are rolling down my face, as I sit writing this evening, even though it's been a little over two months since her passing. It is still very fresh and raw. Having her internment last week opened up the wounds all over again; hoping now we will all find some closure.

I am sticking close to home this summer, as I am needed. My littlest granddaughter and her Dad, my son, are on their own again so helping where and when I can. I must say, it is different so-called babysitting a girl soon to be a teenager. Alas, maybe it's just me getting older, approaching those senior years – the white-haired Grandma?

How I react lately to some things leaves me concerned; I either burst into tears at the heartbreak I see caused by others, or I retreat? Retreating from anything has never been me, so this too causes some wonderment in my thought process. I forgive, but I guess I don't forget the many unkind and thoughtless words directed my way by some siblings and other members of their families – nothing is ever gained by hurting one another. Mom had called us all together late last fall reminding us to all pull together as a family when she was gone – that evening and her laboured words seem to have been all but forgotten. Nothing more can be done, the hurt has gone too far, so I remain friends with a few of my siblings and just avoid the rest. It is far better to avoid the heartbreak which getting together always seems to bring.

I realize lately I have reached a point in my life now where others trivial ways no longer interest me. I have seen a lot in my three score years or so and now prefer to let the dust settle once again, and just be me.

I dropped by for a little visit last night with my friend to just say "Thank you" for those words last summer, "get out there and do what you do best – Volunteer". These words could never have rang clearer than last night when attending an Annual General Meeting here in town for an organization dear to my heart. He had said on many occasions, "you are a people person" – yes, I am. I love connecting with friends, new and old.

Funny how time seems to take care of all – the realization last night as I visited of how content this man is with his life the way it is.

CHAPTER 18

No Closure

The realization that this is not my battle; only he can right the wrongs done him over the years. It is becoming clearer to me now that he has never had closure on the many trials of his life.

How could he let the last one win, I wonder? Is it just easier to retreat for years after all the troubles and live in a dream world of sorts? That way no one gets hurt, no one is allowed in, he just keeps up the façade for as long as possible. Oops, but then you meet "The Writer in Me" and oops, oops, oops …. the real world! She expects a return on the love and affection shown.

I have become mired down once again in other's troubles. I must remember tomorrow and onwards, listen but don't take on their world – it is not your responsibility!

Now, to find that sparkle that used to be so apparent on my face; Where has it gone? Where is it hiding?

CHAPTER 19

Leaving

Mid November 2017 – Decision made! Off again! 2016/17 has pushed me to the brink! Mom has passed away, a relationship with the one I really cared about has turned oh so sour and, volunteering in this town sure has turned out to be not what I thought! Anxious to be on my way, new beginnings – East Coast here I come. Reset/ rejig!

It's in my DNA to adventure for sure, aware of this even more since my husband's passing which gives me pause at the moment to sit and reflect on all those moves with his military career over the years, back and forth across this country.

A meeting from hell tonight, no respect whatsoever for the sitting Board, cutting people off, jeering, yelling, total disrespect. As the Board resigned, and we their friends left the room to the disarray it had become, with the so-called winners taking over, I remained quiet, but I was so disgusted. I no longer want to be part of this organization, with what it has become over the last few weeks. I now realize that it wouldn't have mattered who was at the helm, the previous President, myself or the President displaced this evening, there was no appeasing this group. They would not be happy until they made themselves in charge. People left in tears, other people were bewildered at to what had just happened.

No sleep, so disillusioned! The next morning, there is a feeling of such emptiness. We have brave faces today but this is sure going to sting for a long time to come. How down one can become from the affairs of such an organization. One can feel sapped of all energy and any shred of happiness. It took me almost all day to even begin to come back to myself. So unbelievable and I suppose astonishing to see small town Canada turn on one another. Friends are turning against one another and to achieve what in the end? Everyone had the same goal in mind, at least I thought so. My range of emotions still goes from disbelief to anger to sadness, weeks later. I fear for those who this organization has been a major part of their daily life, and now no longer. What will they do with those now major gaps of empty time in their lives? A friend said she was bruised and aimless for a bit after that meeting – about sums it up. I felt the same, but couldn't put words to it.

The overwhelming blessing from this experience has been the great coming together of friends. An invite to a cottage for a night when most needed, floored me with emotion. These friends knew I was all alone with my feelings and wanted to give me safe haven and a place to talk if needed or just to rest and rejuvenate. Another couple offered me a place to stay whenever needed in the short term or for as long as I wanted, once they found out about my new plans.

Never one to endure boredom too long, I do have a plan, and a whole winter/spring to put it into action! I remember my husband and I had a plan; we were going to get rid of everything upon retiring and travel in the States all winter and then head into Canada spending each summer with the kids. So, we didn't get to do that, but I sure can make another plan. Too often of late, I have seen friends who didn't make it, didn't get to get to their bucket list. I'm not saying I have a bucket list, but, I am inspired to do the thing I love best, rather than just existing the rest of my days. Sixty five plus soon and I will have fun each and every day, whether it's a quiet drive in the country or a rambunctious time out with friends.

Woohoo, yes! That reminds me, time out this Friday evening with friends, must not forget to check my calendar and meet up on time.

Now, it's time to make sure those of importance are told first – then, spring it on the world. She's off and on another adventure, this time one for the rest of her life.

It'll be a year or two maybe in certain locals in this vast country, before ending up closer to my girls in the West. First up - to set my sights on the east coast, and refresh with some old memories of people and places, and to find some new spots to explore this time around as well.

The research and planning begins. There is a lot to think about, first to decide upon the first spot to land and make those accommodation arrangements, disposal of the possessions, whether it be hand off to my children or by way of sell/donate and, then the actual trip.

I head off to bed these nights dreaming of the many possibilities, of what and which to do first, second, third. Time will tell. I love the planning, planner girl I am! Tonight, as I drift off, my head will be full of thoughts of Prince Edward Island and our years there in the 90's; such great times - still have close friends there till this day and can't wait to meet up again. What did I miss doing while there the first time? It's been almost 20 years since we left the Island but I have had a few trips back over the years and have sure enjoyed those visits.

No fear, just my inquisitive nature kicking in now that I've made the decision to do this. I am invincible, always.

The oddest comment hit home today; "well, you dodged that bullet"; hmmm, guess I did, was that a good thing? I guess so, still raw though, doesn't seem to want to leave my heart and soul, not too easily anyways. I do know now time always heals, so can only hope. Letting go will be such a struggle for me, I know. So much unsaid but is it my inner soul just wanting what I want to be?

Oh, what to write in that Christmas card –

Time to purge, purge, purge!

Fall leading up to the Christmas holiday season, busy with an invite to the Grey Cup game here in Ottawa! So fun, so cold a day and such a snowy drive home but so worth it to spend a day with my sister and her husband; something I will never forget. I'd never ever been to a football game in my life and to think I got to go to a Grey Cup in our Nation's capital – a true Canadian tradition!

Christmas parades, numerous birthday parties, visits and phone calls to the elderly and some of my Mom's friends over the holiday season, fill the winter days.

I keep thinking back to a couple of conversations one day visiting some friends that are now shut in. One lady spoke intimately of her feelings after she was left a widow quite young with children to raise. I always had had the greatest respect for this woman (I'd known her all my life) but to hear her speak of the pain she had experienced, I was in awe. The other spoke of my situation and how it could possibly be on the cusp of changing. I am still troubled, sleepless at times, wondering – this is heavy stuff.

The holiday season is upon us and with it the many mixed feelings of Christmas's past. There are deep hurts within my own family since my Mom's passing. No family is immune to this it seems as I speak with others and hear much of the same stories.

I sit in church most Sundays with this overwhelming feeling about this man, that everything will be OK. How, I ask myself, what is the answer? This the strangest of feelings that all will be right in due time, overcomes me most Sundays. I feel myself drift away during the sermon with a clear image of him appearing before my very eyes at the front of that church. I do not understand!

A patient with dementia or Alzheimers often feels lost after supper in the evening, with dusk coming on. I, also feel lost and riddled with a strong feeling of still wanting to connect with this man each evening. Similar in effects, I suppose – me, suffering great love for this man, yet loneliness and the dementia patient suffering the pain of living in the past so clearly but totally lost in the present.

Christmas Eve, 2017 - unknowing flutters in my heart …. Then heartbreak at the end of the evening, never able to break through that wall, I feel so helpless. The hurts done him have lingered over the years, hardening his being and seemingly making it impossible to break through the barrier. Some movement, but what is he thinking? What does he want in the end? Is it the same as me?

I have to keep planning and moving forward as if I am leaving – he has given me no reason to think otherwise. I am now in the process of cleaning my email system, my file cabinet, and actually sending things to the kids. Photo albums and mementos that I am unable to part with will be stored at a daughter's. It is almost surreal now that the time gets closer to turning the calendar to January 2018 that I'm really doing this!

Mid-January, is this all there will be? An evening out with friends and family at a local charity fundraiser, a first I believe in many years – still the same, no sign of any commitment to the future or to me?

Another tune sent my way one evening a week or so later – the deep meaning to the lyrics to these songs sent me baffles me; is it as I've suspected for a long time, his way of truly showing his feelings towards me? It's almost like he's afraid to voice them on his own, lets the music do the talking. This last one has my heart fluttering – what does he want? Once again the ball is in his court at the end of January. I so want to have this chat soon – my plans

45

have been kind of put on hold the past week, till I get a better take on the situation.

I had an interesting chat with an acquaintance on these two experiences with men I've had in the past 5 years. Since she knew of both of them and had lived in this town for years, perhaps she had a better insight than I as to what had happened in both instances or - was it just someone caught up in my drama for an escape from their own? How do they know what is best for me in the long run?

Then I thought about my own vulnerability – the message in the sermon at church today certainly resonated with me in many ways. Is it the opinion of others that once widowed you become vulnerable? Maybe so, certainly not something I would have ever pondered when I was still happily married.

Feb 14, 2018 – a rubbish afternoon and evening, after being ever so brave in posting all is well this morning to my friends on social media. All is well in a sense; it's been so long since my husband's passing now that time has indeed healed. But, the sting of not knowing where I stand with this one man, I love so dearly has again taken its toll. I am troubled, consumed once again as to why things are as they are. A promise to myself this evening to start tomorrow afresh, what will be will be. He knows I need answers and/or closure to this phase of my past, however I do believe he is truly not able to provide that for whatever reason. It's not knowing that whatever reason that will linger with me forever.

End of February, still the visits and the chats over a cup of tea – but no commitment.

Sleepless nights; memories of times he'd wanted to talk late at night and I had listened. I so could've shown up on his doorstep last night and melted into his arms – just the snuggle needed and to know there was someone there for me.

Acquaintances (his and mine) have told me to stay away, getting into more than I need or deserve at this point in my life. Why did no one tell me of this before I got in so deep? Were they hoping that I could fix this man? They should have known only he could fix whatever is troubling him. Ironic, that in my book, Begin Again, I speak of friends who didn't realize that they couldn't fix me after my husband's death; I had to do that for myself.

So, as spring is about to arrive, I take the plunge – I must get away for awhile. I have commitments in the area this summer but nothing holding me back for a few weeks. The tentative plan is to take a road trip East visiting old friends along the way, secure accommodation in Prince Edward Island for the fall and after the summer in Ontario, head back east.

CHAPTER 20

63 Days on the Road and Then Some

First up, a visit back to the area of Nova Scotia where I have lived in the past and love so much. Visiting with old friends, attending Sunday church, lovely meals shared with old friends and neighbours and oh so many oatcakes and tea biscuits for tea; my heart was filled once again with gratitude at the generosity of these folks. An evening out at the local Pub and a time on stage with the Band as per usual was so much fun. It was so refreshing to be back amongst my friends.

Then, I headed straight for the Confederation Bridge linking me to familiar haunts along the way to a friend's cottage in Clinton. A cool spring in PEI but what with a heater warming up the cottage and a lot of laughs and cups of tea, the time there passed away quickly as well. I so enjoyed the simple pleasures of life such as hanging out my laundry on the line in the fresh sea breeze – it was like I was in another world. Numerous trips took place that week as well to the ocean's door. Oh, to look across that blue horizon where the sea and sky seem to meet. It was during this time that quite unexpectedly I came across a newspaper ad with an apartment for rent, so off I went to have a look. After securing that accommodation for the fall, a bit more time was spent sightseeing and revisiting old spots and just enjoying all that spring in Prince Edward Island had to offer.

The following week, I headed for Pictou, Nova Scotia to visit old military friends from our days on Canadian Forces Station Baldy Hughes, located near Prince George, British Columbia. This was a whole new area for me, so had a good explore. After a few days in this area, I realized it was sending the same vibe to me as the Glen Margaret/Hacketts Cove area of NS had just a few years ago. By this I mean the people, the landscape, the culture – so very warm and welcoming.

Then, as I had previously purchased a ticket for a Songwriter's Circle in North Sydney, Cape Breton, off I headed. Not disappointed, as always the drive in Cape Breton was majestic. Bruce Guthro. Lennie Gallant, Heather Rankin and Terry Kelly put on one of the best Songwriter's Circles I've ever had the privilege of attending that evening. I have driven the Cabot Trail in Cape Breton a few times, always an awe inspiring experience, but this time I wanted to explore an area I hadn't been to before, St. Peter's.

I was a little bit early for a visit to Rita MacNeill's Tea Room (season hadn't quite opened yet for business) but wasn't disappointed with the drive. The scenery in Cape Breton is absolutely stunning. I stayed a few days in St. Peter's this time with another friend, who I'd actually made acquaintance with a few years before on a Caribbean cruise. I am blessed to have met the people I have so far in life. Meeting her family and being made most welcome to a Sunday evening supper, attending a birthday luncheon with her friends, going to Bingo one evening and just sightseeing around the area on a lot of back roads, gave me such a flavour of this area. It was hard to leave, but off I went as I was expected at another destination soon.

I arrived at the ferry terminal a little early that afternoon and took a walk about enjoying the sun. I immediately noticed a number of other passengers waiting for the ferry and who were walking about much as I was, although these were mostly couples. I felt a jealous twinge there and then that afternoon, thinking back to how my late husband and I had never enjoyed those retirement years we had so been counting on. The ferry arrived and all of a sudden I found myself driving onto the ferry down in the bottom floor of the boat. All of a sudden, I was petrified! I was driving down but I couldn't see where I was going; ahh, at last the bottom level of the boat. Shaken, I parked the car and found my way to the cafeteria for some food and beverage. I sat there realizing my mood change of the afternoon, saddened. I'd never drove onto a ferry before, let alone down into the jowels of that monstrocity; Ray had always done it. I think back how vulnerable I was that afternoon. Maybe I was just tired from the sheer length of the road trip, realizing how far I'd come from home in the last couple of months or maybe it was because I wasn't quite sure of what the future would hold, now that I'd started on this latest adventure.

I felt better as I landed on the Island once again. I was here and was ready to sit for three weeks or so until time to head back to Ontario for the summer. I am forever grateful for friends at that cottage who allowed me time to sit and think. Lots of trips here and there on the Island filled my days until it was eventually time to head back home, or at least home as I knew it at that moment.

Nearing the end of June it was time to head out. A few days stop in Quebec City to visit a friend and her husband was a nice break. Again, I was made most welcome in their home in the city, was taken around the City on quite a tour, enjoyed some wonderful meals at home and out in the old City and then, off we went for a few days in the country. So refreshing. Now, time to head back to Ontario, my friend from Quebec City coming along with me to deal with some unfinished business she had in Ottawa. I was so grateful for the company, as I was finding it a bit hard now that

I was headed back to Ontario for the summer, not really where I wanted to be but responsibilities called. My driving speed actually slowed after I dropped my friend off in the city and headed towards home? I was dreading what the next couple of months might hold. Unsure, my thoughts full of "what if's" I plugged on.

The first week of July was filled with excitement as all the children and grandchildren and I had a great family gathering at a daughter's home in Calgary, Alberta. Sitting watching my family interact with each other, I realized how quickly these little people, the grandchildren were quickly turning into young adults. I am so very proud of each and every one of them and of each of my three children. The son-in-laws always make me feel welcome, although most time there is a fair bit of teasing, at my expense. I love them all. My next book, actually underway at the moment is a recollection of my life, for my children and grandchildren especially. I want them to know who that blonde haired woman was in her little blue car that kept driving off on another adventure. But, that's a story for another day.

The day of our public school reunion arrived and was quite a success. A good number of people attending, all having a great time getting reacquainted and a good sum of money raised to further the programs of the local museum – success, mission accomplished.

I think back over the summer months and my anxiousness, to just get on with the fall. I did see that fellow a couple of times over the summer, but still things between us remained unchanged. Confusion, I suppose on both our parts as to what I was planning next and if our friendship would endure.

CHAPTER 21

Home, Maybe Not

Fast forward – fall of 2018; I never thought I would be leaving the place I thought home was, so soon after my arrival there two years ago; 3 weeks in, now back on the East Coast I am frustrated a bit still with not being able to see the future – always the girl who has to have at least a short term plan, this is a new experience for me – no real plan; just the change needed to see if I can break the longing for this man and move on with my life. Easier said than done! As I do the address changes, reality is setting in. My mind tells me to keep plugging along, although my heart is still back home. It starts to become easier as I put one foot in front of the other, going for a drive or on an explore. I will stay for a bit, and determine if this is the place for me, or if it is only for a bit. My plan was to try these new adventures; I have to not give up, keep on going.

One of the most important lessons I have learned from this recent decision to shake up my life yet once again – stuff, what is it? Why do we accumulate it? Shedding everything except what would fit in the trunk of my car this time around has been so cleansing – I would rather see material things given to our children and family members if they indeed want it and can use it now, rather than later. I did leave a few things with a daughter that I just wasn't sure of what I wanted to do with just yet, but all in all, I have not missed those things. They are only things. I do realize this lifestyle is not for all, especially not the faint of heart, however it works for me. It affords me the time to write, to read on a variety of subjects and enjoy one of my favourite pastimes – exploring this beautiful country we call Canada – camera in hand.

Something is calling me today across that wide expanse of blue, staring me in the face as I let my bare toes wiggle in that red sand. The adventure is not over by any means, the journey continues.

As always my thoughts intensify during the night – it is nothing for me to wake up with sentences, thoughts, and people and places filtering through until I awaken as if I'm speaking to someone. Up I get to cobble them down on paper, on a regular basis.

Again, where is home? A struggle to answer this question just yet, but I am getting closer. I will always and forever care deeply for this man. Although, my heart and soul remain frozen in time – locked in sorrow at the depth of my loss, I do see a little more clearly this morning – it's like these new adventures for the next while are just stepping stones as I continue along on this journey called life.

AUTHOR'S NOTE

I am indeed resilient, inquisitive, yet also caring. This book is a further chronicle to my life after the trauma of my husband's death, now almost 13 years ago. I share my intimate story with you in the hope it might be a source of encouragement to those going through similar circumstances. Those of us left here on this earth, have the responsibility to live, not just exist. Our loved ones would expect nothing more/nothing less from us.

ACKNOWLEDGEMENTS

Thanks to those that have provided me with support, but mostly inspiration as I travelled this recent journey. Inspiration has come from many people and places, too numerous to mention. A new friend, though sparked my creativity once more this past fall, to finish this manuscript and go to the publishing stage. Thank you, Nancy Lee Amos for giving me that little push needed.

Note: Nancy Lee Amos is also a published author, with three books in the "Isabella" series to her credit.